Once It Stops

Once It Stops

poems

Florence Fogelin

DEERBROOK EDITIONS

PUBLISHED BY
Deerbrook Editions
PO Box 542
Cumberland, ME 04021
www.deerbrookeditions.com

FIRST EDITION

ISBN: 978-0-9904287-7-0

Cover photograph: Rosamond Orford. *Water Colours*. Norwich, VT: Upcountry
Press (2002), reproduced by kind permission of the photographer.

Book design by Jeffrey Haste

for RJF

Contents

For in what does time differ from eternity
but that we measure it?

—Anne Carson

I

Once It Stops

Once it stops snowing
I breathe the color of nothing;
a porous sponge mops the spilled skymilk.

In drifts of small
and shrouds of soft,
doubting the existence of guardrails,

I intuit my way home
to a farmhouse, white embossed on white,
that hangs by a thread of wood smoke.

The Death of Capitalism

Without a care for what it costs
is how she puts it

and that I *must be told*
— as if truth is the salt that sweetens.

When you say goodnight, her laugh
is meant for me.

Winter's spent, still it transacts with spring:
mud season, time to blame the weather.

Balancing words, you say you want me
to spend my life with you —

Midas's treasured daughter, solid as a pot,
dreaming of the house and all it holds in flames:

too many books, too many things.
I smell her cigarettes on your skin.

Rising to toss a log on the fire
you groan at the burden of coins in your pocket.

> *that laugh again . . . nehnehneh neh . . .*
> *Janis Joplin sings* Me and Bobby McGee

Like mourners on a straight-backed bench,
we face the fire as it burns and settles, watch

an ash of paper, freed of words,
lift, pause, and with a shudder vanish.

Here at the Beginning

What is is now, was, and always will be,
world without end, world without beginning.
—Parmenides

We come as pilgrims to a place vacant but for stones.
Here, from the start, we listen
      to wind currying the pines
      to birds saying nothing new
hoping to hear an arrhythmic heartbeat:
stone masons chipping at perplexity.

Strangers in Elea, a birthplace of philosophy,
we seek the old, the new – the difference –
following a path, finding steps.
Beneath our feet, stones showing scant signs of work
but placed skillfully on end and meant to last
remain obdurate.

On this slope of hard light and shadow
we squint into the day's hot dazzle
and scribble in the dirt,
at one with Xenophanes, Parmenides, Zeno,
alive to the paradox: teacher and student.

Voyage to the New World

1

Among the winged, expatriated seeds
blown free in early summer air –
a windswept surge of basic needs,
life's fair share of sun and rain –
should one who travels far and feeds
on perfect light and soil complain –
or boast – about her past and its despair?
Life seemingly begun in flight,
consider herself an interesting epiphyte?
Among fallen acorns risking drought
and rivals, the emigrant will gladly leave
behind her childhood and the family plot,
feeling not the slightest urge to grieve.

2

I knew early on I'd leave the South,
lost my accent right away.
Even close friends don't know where I'm from.
Content to be an alien,
I claim as home any place I choose to be.
Never having belonged,
I love not belonging. I admit it's arrogance
to be defined by travel-thirst.
My mother let me be the first to go;
she didn't get to live anywhere else
but the town she was born in.

3
Among the cadences and pulse of village life,
Tuscany puts me in my place,
humbles me with language, the lack of it,
and liberates strangeness from itself.
Relaxing in a landscape with its own vocabulary,
I step into a past/present/future,
reading under an ancient arbor of newborn leaves,
comforted that my Italian dictionary
has no one word that quite means
home.

Anticipation

I know the devil's tempting me.
Smiling at October, he's braced high
in a scaffold of branches like a stage designer
handing to his assistant, with a wink at me,
errant twigs that interfere with his intent
to make a crabapple tree flower, fruit, fatten, hold
until I lighten things a bit, come next August.
Perhaps I'm a challenge to him: a bender of boughs,
one who picks knowingly toward the tip
to prevent the limb's leaping beyond my highest reach.

He knows what he's doing; his hands are slow.
These things take time, no two the same.
He gives me the eye,
limes the limbs with songs and whistles
and lets me ripen my personal choices –
like Eve, perhaps, or Richard's Lady Anne,
nobody's fool, knowing how it will end,
ensorcelled by the chance to play a part,
to take what's offered.

Leverone Field House

Out in the dark a floodlit waltz of snowfall
takes the breath of men who know its weight,
who shovel walks and tend the indoor track,
now inside leaning on their brooms, a barricade
against a cooling rush of loveliness.

       The girls are limbering up, lithe as cats on tiptoe,
       college girls swinging their soft hair
       brushed to a sheen as lustrous as their sweat.

They watch the girls'
steps and starts, testing and relaxing
into bursts of speed,
firm-fleshed in stain-tight lycra bodysuits,
miracle fibers developed for moon- and space-walks.

       Pastel paddles, they stir 'round and around
       in this bowl set out in snow.

The men talk of hunting deer, circling the prey
and fishing through an eyelet in the ice:
the catch that rises out of summer,
spiraling up to an aching, ungloved hand.

       Stretching out of the turn, footsteps
       beating like a bird's heart, throats exposed,
       breasting imagined tape, shoulders trailing victory,
       free of terror.

Coming up Threes

Your eyes are seriously blue,
so when you locked your gaze on me and,
less than three months old,
wouldn't let me look away,
I wondered if they'd keep their claim
on me and on the sky.

Now you're three, well-traveled,
word- and worldly-wise.
I cannot see myself in you:
you're a boy,
my eyes are almost green.

Seven decades separate the two of us,
but we agree that the world is of serious interest.
Watching apples growing on a tree.
Watching them fall. Counting to three.

Housekeeping

In the kingdom of Illyria —
call it Aspalathos, Dalmatia, Yugoslavia, Croatia —
men with dusty feet are hefting blocks
already hewn to size, some with partial inscriptions.
Such are the uses of the past: upkeep.
Historians remain: jailed and jailers
living in the heavy, August-heat-drenched walls
of Diocletian's Palace.

Today's familiar chore
is rearranging unmatched stones, matching them
to this year's purpose:
bits of Rome, Byzantium, last year's pig sty,
the cell of a medieval monk
freshly pocked with bullet-holes.
A young woman steps, with a basket on her hip,
from a Roman garrison
to hang out baby clothes with red plastic clothespins,
looks at tourists passing,
and pushes a damp curl beneath her braid.

Vantage Point

The very "there-you-are-and-where-are-you"
of poetry itself.
— Seamus Heaney

Chanterelles.
        It's easy picking to spot
their salmon-orange glow, their holy robes
of saffron lifting from the musty soil,
their apricot-smell in the rain. Jeweled with dew
among rotten leaves, they're as unlikely as tropical coral
would be rooted here on a reef in New Hampshire,
near where Frost chose to make a home.
I sat on his porch with a yellow pad and pencil,
enjoying a late summer afternoon,
the wind's slow breathing, a familiar view.
        Is place, this place, or any other place
        what's needed for a creative life?

*****

I found *North of Boston* on a shelf
when we bought our lakeside cottage
twenty miles or so from where he shunned
living a purely literary life –
days writing words derived from words.
        No ideas but in things?
        No, no ideas but in verbs.
When he watched stars it was to see
them move: to timeclock Orion
as he clambered over the hill and crossed the sky.

His stars still burn, the constellations pivot.
My son built his own Star Splitter;
he'd rouse us from sleep to trace asteroids
and wouldn't let us miss Northern Lights
shimmering with their otherworldliness.
      A place is where there's something going on.

*****

But why on earth did he move *here* from England?
New Hampshire doesn't convey how cold it is!
The wonder is he found the place congenial:
remote, the soil so poor, the house so small.
      It's welcoming, I'm told,
        but trembles in the night as if it might
        surrender as so many others have
        and fall to ruin in its own cellar hole.
Gone is his window tree; the elms are gone.
He left this house, moved again and again.
I'm shadowed as I walk from room to room.
Safe on the porch, I'm glad to be alone
and escape a roof deformed by years of snow.

*****

I spend a lot of time talking to myself;
for me, the question's *how* to live, not where.
What's needed is a nomad's telescope
and a vantage point –
      to slow the dizzy spinning of the world
      to see the stars outnumber our concerns
      and watch water dripping in a crevice.
For this and more, the farmhouse served him well.

Not me. I'm just passing by, come
to fill my plastic bottle from his spring,
to take away a flower, a chanterelle,
or better yet a piece of quartz, a stone
durable, rough . . .
I climb his hill the better to be alone:
to find the wherewithal
to chisel verbs on a summer-cloud balloon.

Geometry Lesson

To see a rhomboid, born at dawn,
cross my bedroom wall from left to right,
a slow-motion Euclidean butterfly,
is to admire as a mathematician might
the beauty of the calculations that inform
the beauty of the world: the angle of the light
foreshortened as its bright wings ply
into an origami in the corner,
a chrysalis from which no sooner free
than rising day pins it to the floor,
extinguishing what one might hope to learn
from its descending flight.

II

Racing the Wrecking Ball

Frederick the Great made history,
          whatever that is,
leaving behind the music he wrote,
not great, not bad, still played,
          the breath still his,
written for a flute that outlasted Prussia.

A tangled curl of candle smoke
          loses itself in the maw of air,
Homer's voice is silent, Sappho's songs in tatters.
Buntings and flags, incense, prayers – ?
          gone without a trace.
Archaeologists poke around in stuff that doesn't rot,
          not yet, anyway.
Historians have what wasn't burned at Alexandria,
paper crumbling to the touch, fading photographs,
generations of orphans
from short-lived technologies.

I have a solid memory:
          round hay bales
standing in for segments and columns of a Greek temple
tumbled not by earthquake but design
and destined to be forage.
          Stone cylinders
last longer, strewn around the quarry
near the ruins of Selinunte,
some half-formed, still rooted in the rock.
They testify to eternal hope seen in every graveyard:
          staying power.
I once owned a cardboard throne.

Gulley Jimson was on to something,
living in a place condemned,
painting murals while he raced the wrecking ball,
                creating shards,
furiously at work in the midden.

The Best of Company

The power and the glory
of a June morning is pushing eighty on I-91 listening
to Glenn Gould play Bach's fifth partita
much too fast – both of us –
each note as articulate as a leaf
in summer's green, hilarious profusion.
The Deity's extravagant, not at all put off by speed.

Zooming into Vermont
I'm in the best of company, an apprentice
learning from masters to focus on detail.
Leaves unfurl, a plethora; I phrase them into trees,
dial up the volume and weave through traffic's
pop tunes, rock, and melodies. Make way!

Make way for the Baroque.
Glory be to God who does things to excess.
Our eyes are programmed *three times over*
to see what He's doing.
Celebrate abundance, abundantly precise.
Step on the gas
and race the sun toward light's longest day.

A Legacy of Spoons

Her mother's vase and her engagement ring
went to me. Little else claimed
more than usefulness, but we divided
things as best we could: kitchenware,
chairs and tables, scarves and pocketbooks,
wondering that she kept so little,
let so much go – a curious virtue,
the arrogance that in themselves things
meant nothing, were never good enough.
It was as if she carried to her grave
a childhood fantasy of having been
the daughter of the czar,

                              and so our sons,
who swarmed around and brought friends, subjects
proud to hold her interest and be valued
over things that break, inherit nothing
but a gyroscope – an attitude
that tests and trues itself – and hand-me-downs
from the realm she ruled:
spoons worn flat from stirring.

Travel Insurance

If this is Earth, why is most of it water —
deep and devouring?
Any Greek could have told Odysseus:

Don't cross Poseidon. Placate him
with a bull, drown your best black horse;
for god's sake give him what he wants!
Take a voyage take a chance you won't come back
is how they saw it. Strange
how many fishermen and sailors
never learn to swim. If you survive

the splash, the silence,
pop the tab. You'll float — two minutes? five?
The flight attendant
makes it sound like a day at the beach,
hypothermia better, far, than drowning.
Before you go,

light the dinner candles,
rub the cat nine times and comb your daughter's hair.
Perform the rituals of sex with your wife.
Like any right-minded man, leave home
with a heavy heart
and a pinch of dirt for luck.

Sisters

Beneath the surface, under the freckles
and sunburned, peeling skin that left my shoulders
looking like a map – so fascinating to me then –
I was growing like a soft-shelled crab, inside out.
Tall and proud of it.
Each time I cut my hair I thought I made it grow,
and when I skinned my knees roller-skating
I lifted up the scab and peeked
to see the future.

Now of course I'm plainly marked
by what I've done, marvel at the scars that fade,
cherish those that don't. The doctor takes my sins away.
He says, *Don't worry but the little angry red ones*
are malignant. Not melanoma . . .
Melanoma, such a pretty name.

My sister died young. She never had a chance
to lose her peaches-and-cream complexion.
She faces me in all the ads and rows of skin-care products:
rub it on and lift your face,
make your liver spots and crow's-feet disappear.
Salves for night, creams for day,
ointments, balms, emollients . . . royal jelly?

I laugh out loud and think of her:
how we used to go to the drugstore
to see the painted lady wearing falsies and mascara,
the only woman in town without eyelid-colored eyelids.
We had gravel in our knees – I still do. Strange

that hers is in some crematorium.
Maybe I could use this stuff.
She'd agree, my stained hide is as tough
as the sloughed bark of a eucalyptus tree
straining against itself,
too big for its britches, still growing.

Window Washing

What we cannot speak about we must pass over
in silence.
— L. Wittgenstein

A warm November day bookmarked
the change of seasons. We washed the windows,
one in, one out, eased into a rhythm and sequence
ending with them walled tight between us
and the coming winter.
One hand wiped past the other's and tapped
at things wanting attention. Sometimes
it takes a change of focus to see what's obvious.
We smiled more than usual; job done,
without a word you kissed my eyes.
January's traceries, with hands steadier than ours,
will etch incremental, feathered proofs of love
on multifaceted canvasses we've prepared,
gessoed with separate-sided care,
each pane an abstract expression
of illuminated silence.

Art Lesson

Children, if you dare to think
Of the greatness, rareness, muchness,
Fewness of this precious only
Endless world in which you say
You live, you think of things like this:
— Robert Graves

I thought it had something
to do with the war, with
the serious, distant
importance of things
my parents talked about
at dinner, the years it
would take for the righting
of wrongs, and the world

never to recover,
when Miss Bell handed us
two sheets of paper – two – each.
The second was only to use if
we made a mistake,
had to start over.
She said, *Springtime. Draw me*
a picture of spring.

Our ration of paper
made what we were doing
seem vital, the paper important itself.
It wasn't as slick
as our usual newsprint;
hay-colored and bumpy,
its texture gave welcome to green,
to the sweep of grass,

to my crayon, the flat side.
I knew grass grew first
in ruts from the plow,
that it snuck under tufts
of old straw still left
in the field, that by skipping
along on the surface
like that, like a stone,

I had done it: the opposite,
and made spring's effect.
And spring was indifferent
so what did I care? –
yellow/green; flower/leaf.
Color and I made grass grow.
My wintered-over field came
alive as I plowed it

with crayons, now feverish
to end – artist,
farmer, warrior combined.
And I'd done it myself! The enemy
code, the secret of artists,
the source of their silence –
all mine. I slowed
to a stop.

Miss Bell found it *different*,
lacking tulips, daffodils, trees . . .
I hated its sight!
It was waxy. It should
have been thin. It lacked air.
The beginning of spring
gone too far –
into summer . . .

I still had the sheet
I'd kept in reserve,
but waste wasn't loyal,
a war going on . . . Odd
to see art as a serious thing,
a world wrapped in paper.
What makes a child dare
untie the string?

Sappho Says

Mary was out in the backyard reading
(I've always wondered what)
when a guy flew over the wall!
You know the story: he was wearing wings.
And Mary:
jeans? shorts? a sundress?
or perhaps her best blue diaphanous gown,
an aspiring Virgin Queen waiting to be discovered.
          What would Sappho say?

The shrink says
dress is of no interest in his therapy.
His wife, handsome in black with white hair
tight in a bun, has the carriage of a ballerina.
He's an aging dandy,
a silk scarf knotted at his neck.
You look like you're in mourning for your sex life,
Peter O'Toole told his wife, tossing her clothes –
mauve, grey, and brown – out into the rain.
          What would Sappho say?

We sat together on the subway,
a couple of catty old women people-watching,
pretending to be sociologists,
when Mnasidica got on at 68th Street:
slim in her jeans and a pink t-shirt,
          PRINCESS
in capital letters glittering on her chest,
black lashes, pink blush, a double twist of pink elastic
wrapped around her brow and ponytail.
Sappho said:
Surely even the glance of the blessed Graces
Is more drawn to whatever is dressed with flowers
Than to the ungarlanded.

Rescue I

In our power are opinions, movement
toward a thing, desire . . .
— Epictetus

Stilled mid-stroke in a sudden moist velour,
queasy, lost, fog-blind — nowhere
the certainties of sea, horizon, air.
Without support nothing counts as sure.

Gulls, hungry-eyed, search each whorl,
my longings emptied out from either oar,
spiraling thoughts absorbed, absorbing more,
that disappear in a flat, fluid world.

A foghorn sounds; a hush surrounds the sun.
Denied by mist, I gain the wind, the sense
and slip of tide, the blind man's recompense
of seeing more than sight would seize upon.

Fullvoiced, it frees my strokes, my soul's long wings,
pulse, desire: the power movement brings.

Al Museo della Storia di Scienza

Io. Europa. Ganymede. Callisto.
Since Galileo hadn't given names,
hadn't pondered naming, he thought first of
trick glass, funny parlor games,
a Dutchman's toy, the kind of thing that's good
for finding ears on Saturn, or the pox that maims
the surface of the moon. Perhaps it could
elaborate God's sky, enrich His claims
wherever the eye of man, empowered, aims.

But more, far more. A disobedient sky
drawn by moons of Jupiter. What do
those circles circle – Godlessness? The eye
must shine that sees the universe anew . . .
Among his notes and telescopes, I try
to find the mind of man that could eschew
the beauty of it, publicly, then vivify
his "Still, earth moves." (Why care? He knew.)
For such as he, what reliquiae will do?

Idols offend; synecdoche annoys.
I know a man whose sperm is worth the fight,
he says, to freeze two hundred years, rejoicing
in his DNA. Bones incite
the faithful. The brain in a vat. Bentham, no voice
but on boxed display and here, an uncontrite
follower made a cheerful graveside choice:
his upthrust middle finger preserved airtight.
A gesture outlasts a Pope: *You see? I was right!*

Contact Sheet

1

The blind man bares his teeth;
someone told him it would do the trick.
Put a quarter in his cup;
watch him try to grin.

2

The little girl, the pretty one,
stops her tears, disappointed
of desired effect.
She frames her mouth to look like lipstick.

3

Lips as grave and tired
as her Picasso-face resting on her elbow,
the woman on the F train holds the baby close
and eats him with her eyes.

4

They're old: not much to say
while they chew, carefully, the early-bird special.
Negotiating coats and doors, they leave behind
their hands, semaphores of caring.

5

Shoulder to wrist to hand . . .
Her expression floats and hovers near her fingertips.
I wish I could dance. I wonder what I look like
when I look at her?

6

She takes the mind/body problem
seriously. I'm working on it my way,
trying to smile, trusting it
to speak for me.

III

Who Is Sylvia?

Oh Lord, let me be
this, this solely:
no longer me
but Sylvia Poggioli.

Famous Poet Returns to Read in Her Hometown

You're lovely as you read, polished,
every inch the poet, dressed of course in black,
teeth diamond-hard with pain.
Your pearls, you say, are a metaphor
for mother's milk chafing your collarbone.
Your smile is not very nice.

O, but the words – they rake the room
like weaponry, strobe lights for the ear.
Glittering like a disco ball, you slice into
your dying father's eyes: improvement came,
you say, by changing each occurrence of *love*
to *hate*, a fingertip command.
Your manner is gentle, memory precise.
I'm glad I'm not your sister.

You pause. I watch your hands
tremble with a glass of water;.
The crowd waits, breathing out and in
in unison. No, it isn't easy;
even words unsaid can kill. Have you been flayed
by shards of someone else's mirror?
How I envy you.

Your voice is not a pretty thing;
you use it like a drill, head down, hard at work
exposing secrets to the sun, the father's unholy ghost.
Words made flesh, hands bloody.

If the Eye Were an Animal

My father's eyes
were pale, unclouded, his pupils irised out
by glaucoma medication.
He had the vacant look of the blind,
yet sight struggled through the aperture
as if for breath. I wondered if he saw me
upside down, as in a camera obscura,
or through a cyan gel.
On misty days, I think of him,
how patiently he took the loss.

Once in a glider
I played tag with a hawk: riding a thermal
we claimed a double helix,
but soaring didn't make me see any better.
And if the clouds lift,
even on Mount Washington, what of it?
If the eye were an animal,
Aristotle said, sight would be its soul.
I don't know how far I want my soul to travel.

Ancient Needs

Sexual complicity in conflict with individual
freedom is a central theme of the Balanchine
pas de deux ...
— Arlene Croce

Two do not become one naturally;
the story's lifelong and complicated.
The Greek idea of creation of the sexes
describes their ancient origin: a single sphere
halved, the desire and need for the missing other.

Wedded in a Möbius strip,
our hands twist two-in-one, inside-out and backwards,
fingers intertwined, not knowing which
is whose and whose to wriggle. How close
is close enough?

You alone understand
my need to separate our tangled selves
and face you, *terre à terre*,
complicit with hands I want not to lift
but let me rise.

Let Them Be Left

I'm back from places picture-perfect:
Tuscany, a sunlit dream
where every hill town punctuates its presence
with double rows of cypress trees
trim as exclamation points.
Back to Partridge Lake,
its spring-fed, snow-filled, muddy wet.

From Italian gardens and city boulevards
defined and caged by geometry –
hedges, topiary, pear trees splayed against a wall,
walks swept impossibly clean, even dirt and gravel.
Back to where the soil's so poor
it needs a granite bed to hold the lake in place.
No one planned this mix of pine, birch, and hardwoods
quarreling for a patch of light,
strangling rocks in search of food so scarce
ancestral rot is nourishment.

In this wild, wet clearing in the woods,
the undergrowth welcomes me home with strangeness:
the smell of a mushroom, the careless ease of ferns.

Rescue II

We went straight out, the morning
was that clear and windless,
ninety degrees off our normal along-the-shore,
the Emerald City close enough to reach for.
Our boats paralleled each other and the Berkeley pier,
the stubs of it remaining. The oar blades
sliced into water that seemed heavier,
more resistant the farther we went,
feeling the pull, the nearness, the depth
of what we worked against.

      Queasy at the summit of a Mayan pyramid,
      anxiety teetering between desire and fear,
      poised in the emptiness of vertigo:
      unable to come down.
      Jump or fall?

Again that terror: The gut. The heart. Paralysis.
      No . I don't know . No . Just talk to me . . .
His voice was my lifeline.
It nudged my shell, as slowly as an oil tanker, pencil-thin,
to turn under the touch of my left oar responding
to my wrist barely moving. Puddling.
How little it took from me
to feel movement before I even wanted it,
to lapse into the rhythm:
release –   recover –   catch –   drive –

      repeat   repeat   repeat

Journey Into Space

You think you know what you're doing:
another great adventure,
like heading out around the world alone.
You've learned the mind's loneliness,
the joys and terrors of the fractional
becoming fully one.
You've learned to sail.

But you don't know where you're going:
one and one = two
on a double one-way ticket
God-knows-where-to.
Who can predict the trajectory of binary stars
dancing their braided ways through space,
the steps and stops of the music of the spheres
played on a guitar?

Something more than one + one:
you've charged the space between you
with light and energy, the force field
where you've now begun your journey.
And have arrived.
May you live deeply in each place and moment.
We pray that you may simply live together simply.

Learning to Walk Again

Without encouragement
or waiting arms to catch them when they fall,
they're learning how to walk
down the street, in the mall, through the park:

slouching, buttless boys who somehow manage
to keep their pants on, oversized and baggy,
as if their enlarged fruit is way too big,
as much a problem as their size 11 feet;

and girls with secrets on display,
learning to cantilever breasts and bums,
when walking tall turns them into jailbait,
stumbling a bit, pointing at the boys

who pointedly don't notice.
The boys shoot hoops and miss;
the girls collapse into each other,
their legs wobbly with exaggerated laughter.

Miss Rome 2000

She's looking good,
dark and slim and smiling,
selling ice cream near the Pantheon.
It's hard to say how long she's been here:
long enough that guys drinking coffee
seem to know her and appreciate
her private reveries, humming quietly,
barely moving to the music on the radio,
aware that they are watching.
She stirs her ass stirring up
gelato, large pastel trays of it,
lavish with attention
to each flavor's swirl and creaminess,
but when she hears a favorite song
she dials the volume up, lifts her arms
like a goddess or a statue
and sings out the refrain:

I'm going to live forever . . .

IV

Pathetic Fallacy

I never believed it anyway,
the notion that the heavens weep when we do,
the sun shines on happiness.
The bluest-ever day in September
was 9/11.

Fall has splashed its energy along the highway leading
to the rehab center, but rain and drizzle
have disappointed this year's leaf-peeping tourists.
Unlike me, they take it personally.

      My grip on the steering wheel is tense, tighter
      than his on the walker he's learning to guide.
      I bring him a shaggymane from our lawn,
      a gift from the world – damp, still without frost.

Reds and golds have printed dark photograms
on wet roads and sidewalks; the oak leaves
refuse to let the weather get them down.

      In diminished light and pouring rain,
      we drive home through shades of brown
      glowing from within,
      rich mahogany to burnished, papery tan.

Time Out of Mind

Our fathers worked in the shipyard,
its siren measuring the decades
at seven, twelve, and four, Monday through Friday.
Church bells claimed Sundays.

The boy the janitor chose to ring the school bell
got respect. At ten-to-nine and ten-to-one
he'd rope us in. A year meant a grade and a teacher,
the future an eternity away.

For graduation we were given watches
no one had needed until then.
How sweet the tick . . . and the delicate touch
it took to wind the stem.

Hardly ever noticed, they've become
battery-driven bracelets. Schedules
no longer measure our days, our years;
the future is an eternity away.

La Dolce Vita in Soho

Champagne and sushi served to celebrate
the opening: Italian lamps and tables,
kitchen faucets, showerheads, all designs worthy
of the Museum of Modern Art.
While Prada-clad models and multilingual businessmen
murmured their admiration of one another's posture,
I tried to imagine them living here,
brushing their teeth, spilling milk, luxuriating
in a travertine tub worth thousands.
Among polished smiles and surfaces of chrome and stone,
a handful of peonies, hung-over and disheveled,
relaxed their blush-pink, blowzy heads
over the sharp edge of a square glass bowl.

The Leveler

. . . the dumb old words that everyone . . .
Eventually must resort to: "I love you," the Leveler.
— John Hollander

Even Shakespeare laments how hard it is
(in sonnet after sonnet, so it can be done)
to make passion new.
As if it ever matters
how many times a play has been performed.

The way we talk, you and I,
is contact sport played for keeps:
thrust and parry, volley and block,
aim, deflect, pause – commonplaces
but for timing. Tone of voice.
Knowing when to laugh.

I love you – I love you – Dumb, of course,
but who needs coded, highfalutin' language?
We understand each other perfectly
and share an appetite for words,
eating them like buttered bread.
A private language isn't possible
and who would want one anyway?

All Men Are Mortal

∴
the
sign of
therefore,
of the cold logic
of why and what we
remember, what brought
us here: another war memorial,
another slant on death, the dead piled
into another pyramid, their names pressed
with salted fingers into granite. They were men;
all men are mortal. Did you think they'd live forever?
Between the *why* and *therefore* falls the shadow.

South and north of here,
on Southern courthouse lawns and Yankee greens,
black cannonballs kiss as much as need demands,
                one
             on three
          three on six
        six on ten & so on
death on death, as deliberate as a war's careful explanation:
        Reasons. Premises. Conclusion.
Washington's smooth face expresses a way to remember,
        a why to forget.

the arc in the envelope

for Ellsworth Kelly

a slice of the horizon
    complete

against the available sky
    lifts open

        space

where the line ends
    where it begins

Forget and Forgive

An anonymous note with return address,
an over-the-transom *Remember me?*
reminds me that the best revenge
lets nature let go:
sentence diagrams without their words – skeletons,
like November's trees whose fallen leaves are blank,
even when I turn them over.
Leave it alone, my mother said.
The scab remains for a reason.

In storage, library card catalogues'
little empty drawers still have metal rods
tying down their lack of information.
Books I've lost, given away,
and still I have too many. It feels good
to go to the dump; I don't regret what's there.
Memory's my friend with soft, aging hands.
Names are first to go –
as if the book's index has gone missing.
Then the plot.

The Boathouse: A Love Poem

Once we walked on water
on winter ice thick enough
to support a demolition job.
The boathouse had to go,
a matter more of disuse than of woodrot.
It was a kind of shared therapy
tearing it apart with our gloved hands,
sledgehammers, crowbars – rough
tools attacking a task with leverage
allowed only by winter's floor.

Removing stubborn, rusty nails,
we heard the children's summery squeals;
no swallows were around to swing by and complain.
We peeled down to our undershirts,
sweating an out-of-season sweat
that defied the icy slush beneath our feet,
boots skittering in awkward navigation.

We made a fire
in snowdrifts burying the beach;
roasted nails remained as evidence
until we mopped them up with magnets.
Like love-crazed fireflies, sparks rose
to celebrate the cold coming of the night,
while the exposed frame leaned
with the loss of its clapboard skin,
one way, then another.
For as long as we could we kept it aright,
swaying and holding on to itself
like a pair of weary marathon dancers.

Finale

The conductor pushes the tempo,
hurrying things along:
violinists pitched forward, leaning on their bows;
the wind section tense, waiting for his nod;
shining cymbals raised for the climax.
        It's not like that. Not a crescendo.

It's more like the day we didn't climb Mt. Jefferson,
our favorite, the summit now too daunting.
We reached tree line and settled
for a picnic on a sunny outcropping
while a white-throated sparrow sang in the boreal scrub,
Mozart's second-movement bird,
music in a minor key, like crystals
growing on a string.
He concentrated stillness with plaintive clarity
appropriate to our suspended place and time, a solo
Old Sam Peabody, Peabody, Peabo . . .
        We felt the space he left behind
        but didn't see him fly.

In Black

Before you go, I want to tell you nothing
of my grief. That will be my business:
the night shift.
Days I will mourn in black —

black for remembering
the heat you gather in your hands
and share with my body.
I'll mourn for you in black
bikini underpants and choose the black brassiere
with its caressing satin sheen.

I'll point my toes and step
into my old black jeans, zip them
over the softness of my belly
and feel your touch in the tightness of the weave.

I'll pull on a turtleneck sweater
I've never been without,
ribbed to hug me as I breathe, made to make the best
of my two best features. I was wearing one
the night we met and got your attention.
My soft Italian boots are in the attic;
sensible shoes will have to do. I'll wear
the soft black leather coat
you insisted that I buy in Florence.

I want to sweat your passing,
feel the moon's passion for the sun
at the moment of eclipse,
alone in seeing that the sun is still shining.
Or become the black cloud that draws the sun
so close its light splays behind her.

Out of Season

Three small red bouquets,
half-pint baskets of strawberries placed
to tempt me on a snowy night
at the counter of the general store,
are doing their best to make me think of June.
It's not their price that puts me off,
but something's wrong:
berries out of season – is it their stinginess?
My future father-in-law liked my greed,
my never-mind-the-dirt, barefoot in his berry patch.
It's not that I do not admire a single rose,
but all in all, I much prefer a bunch.
Spring is not a gesture,
                              which is just to say
I will not eat the berry that's been counted
sooner than I'd live life one day at a time.

c.v. of a poet

It only seems
that I have not been
in a single line of work:
student, teacher, historian,
mother, management-trainee,
writer, editor,
mistress
of the classroom, a college, many kitchens,
wife, lover, friend.
Always a translator
of English into English.

Acknowledgments & Notes

Acknowledgments

Grateful acknowledgment is made to the following publications in which these poems, some in different versions, have appeared:

Poet Lore. "The Art Lesson"

Cumberland Poetry Review. "Famous Poet Returns to Read in Her Hometown"

The Lyric. "Rescue I"

2001: A Science Fiction Poetry Anthology. "Al Museo della Storia di Scienza"

Starving Romantics Poetry Competition (third prize). "Voyage to the New World", Part I

Porter Gulch Review. "Geometry Lesson"

Birchsong: Poetry Centered in Vermont. "Scapes"

Oyster Boy Review. "The Best of Company"

Press 53 2013. "Racing the Wrecking Ball," "Rescue II," and "Housekeeping"

The Florida Review. "Once It Stops"

Websites:

Womensvoicesforchange.org. "Housekeeping," "Contact Sheet," and "c.v. of a poet"

PoetryDaily.com. "Once It Stops"

Poems included in the chapbook *Facing the Light,* published by Redgreene Press (2001): "All Men Are Mortal," "Famous Poet Returns to Read in Her Hometown," "Miss Rome 2000," "Rescue I," "If the Eye Were an Animal," "Sisters," and "Window Washing."

Dedications

"Voyage to the New World" is dedicated to the Palazzolo family of Siena; "Coming up Threes" to Oliver Fogelin, my grandson; "Travel Insurance" to Patricia Jaeger; "Journey into Space" to my sons and their wives; "Vantage Point" to the Frost Place, Franconia, New Hampshire, in recognition of its nurturing environment.

Thanks

The cover photograph is from *Water Colours,* by Rosamond Orford (Upcountry Publishing, 2002; www. upcountrypublishing.com). Jeffrey Haste, Deerbrook Editions editor and publisher, made the book a reality. My warmest thanks to them both.

I am grateful to W. W. Cook and to the memory of Richard Eberhart, Amy Clampitt, and John Engels, fine poets and helpful friends. Mark Cox helped me focus (and shorten) "Vantage Point." The Still Puddle Poets have given close readings with friendship and laughter. April Ossmann helped my editing in every way; Bronwyn Becker was my copy editor. For a lifetime of love and things to write about, my greatest debt is to Robert Fogelin.

Notes

(p. 24) "Vantage Point," set at the Frost Place, is marked throughout by borrowings from Frost's poetry. Footnotes would mar the pleasure of finding the correspondences for oneself. The epigraph is an excerpt from "Electric Light" in *Electric Light* by Seamus Heaney. Copyright © by Seamus Heaney. Reprinted by permission of Farrar, Strauss and Giroux LLC.

(p. 33) In "The Best of Company," reference is made to a claim in the *New York Times* that the eye has three kinds of receptors, all of which see the color green.

(p. 39) "The Art Lesson" begins with an epigraph from Robert Graves's "Warning to Children."

(p. 42) "Sappho Says" concludes with a Sappho translation by Josephine Balmer.

(p. 53) "Let Them Be Left" owes its title to a line in "Inversnaid" by Gerard Manley Hopkins. Its former title was "Scapes."

(p. 64) "The Leveler" derives its title and epigraph from John Hollander's "Considered Speech" in *Picture Window*.

About the Author

Florence Fogelin's first published poem appeared in *Negative Capability* on the recommendation of Richard Eberhart. Subsequent poems have appeared in *Poet Lore*, the *Cumberland Poetry Review*, *The Lyric*, and other journals. "Once It Stops," her title poem, was featured on the *Poetry Daily* website, following publication in *The Florida Review*.

Her chapbook, *Facing the Light*, was said by John Engels to be "elegant work, direct, unaffected, eloquent and passionate." She has been a finalist for the Gell Prize by Writers & Books and a semifinalist for Word Works' Washington Prize. Three poems were included in the *Press 53 Open Awards Anthology 2013*, one of which was featured – with two others – by the website: womensvoicesforchange.com.

A graduate of Duke University with masters degrees from Yale University and Claremont Graduate School, Fogelin has written and edited publications at Yale University and Dartmouth College. A resident of Vermont, she organized a reading at the St. Johnsbury Athenaeum by twenty poets from *Birchsong: Poetry Centered in Vermont*, in which her work appeared. Married to a professor of philosophy, she has three adult sons.